The Absolute Beginner's Guide to the New York Subway

By Minh T. Nguyen

The Absolute Beginner's Guide to the New York Subway
by Minh T. Nguyen

First Edition: October 2013
www.nycsubwayguide.com

ISBN: 978-1-304-58273-7

To PT

My adventures in the city are never complete without you

Contents

.

Introduction

Let's face it — the most convenient, cost-effective way to travel in New York City is by subway. For many first-time visitors, tourists, and even locals, however, the complexity of the system can be very intimidating and confusing.

Time and time again, I see tourists step on the wrong train, wonder why a train does not stop at their desired destination, or become stranded at some station with no clue where to go.

I don't blame them. The New York subway system is not the simplest in the world. What many native New Yorkers take for granted can be very confusing and unintuitive to outsiders.

Seeing so many visitors struggle with the system, I decided to write a guide to set them at ease. I make absolutely no assumptions about what you know about taking public transportation in New York and explain how to use it from top to bottom, sometimes in excruciating detail. I've added a lot of photos to help illustrate the subway system. My goal is to make an easy-to-read, step-by-step guide that allows you to overcome your fear and frustration with taking the trains and maximize your time and money while you are here.

I very much welcome your suggestions, feedback, and corrections. Please e-mail me if you have ideas on how to improve this guide.

Cheers,
Minh T. Nguyen
minh@minh.org

New York, October 2013

Understanding the basics

Before I delve into the details of how to take the trains, let me help you understand some of the basic information about the system.

What is the New York City subway system?

The subway system is the main public transportation system in New York. It is one of the oldest and largest public transportation systems in the world (in terms of number of stations). With some 5.4 million riders on a given weekday, it is one of the primary modes of transportation for the majority of New Yorkers and tourists. The system is operated by the Metropolitan Transportation Authority (MTA).

The subway system is usually just referred to as the "trains." Locals say "I can take the train to your place" to generally mean that they take the subway. **The subway is never referred to as the *metro, underground, or tube.***

Unless noted otherwise, I mean the subway system if I just use the word *train* by itself. While trains mostly run underground in Manhattan, a good portion of trains run at ground level or on elevated tracks in the other boroughs.

What is not the New York City subway?

While the subway system is the primary mode of transportation in New York, it is not the only transportation system in the greater metropolitan area. Other large, train-based transportation systems that you should not confuse with the New York subway include the following:

- AirTrain JFK/Newark
- Amtrak
- Long Island Rail Road (LIRR)
- Metro-North Railroad
- New Jersey Transit
- Port Authority Trans-Hudson (PATH)

With the exception of the AirTrains, these trains are referred to as "commuter trains" because commuters from outside New York take these to commute in and out of the city on a daily basis. This book does *not* apply to any of these transportation systems.

To avoid confusion, most locals refer to these transportation systems by their names. They'll say, "I'm taking the Metro-North this weekend," "Let's take the New Jersey Transit to the airport," or "I'm coming in from the PATH train." Remember, the word *train* by itself without any other designation is usually reserved for the actual New York subway.

Understanding New York City's geography

New York City is divided into five boroughs:

The subway system operates in all five boroughs.[1] It never leaves New York City. You have to take one of the commuter trains mentioned previously to do so.

The boroughs are often used as a direction of travel for trains:

- Trains that travel towards Manhattan are **Manhattan-bound** trains
- Trains that travel to Brooklyn are **Brooklyn-bound** trains
- Trains that travel to Queens are **Queens-bound** trains

etc.

---

[1] The Staten Island Railway on Staten Island does not officially belong to the subway system, even though it shares the same farecard and is depicted on subway maps

There is no physical train connection between Staten Island and the other boroughs. You have to take the ferry or cross a bridge to get to Staten Island. However, once you are on Staten Island, you can ride the trains there just as you do everywhere else (without paying more or buying another farecard).

Manhattan's street grid

The street system in Manhattan is composed of a rectangular street grid. Streets travel east and west, while avenues travel north and south.[2] Street numbering increases as you go further north, while avenue numbering increases as you go further west:

This grid system is not perfect. For instance, there is no 4th Ave. (it's known as Park Ave. instead) and the grid system does not really exist below 14th St. However, the concept of this grid suffices for now. Keep this concept in mind as it will help you find subway stations and navigate maps.

---

[2] This is not entirely accurate, since the grid system is not perfectly aligned with the directions on the compass.

Understanding Uptown, Midtown, and Downtown

Roughly speaking, Manhattan can be divided into three areas:

- Uptown (anything north of 59th St.)
- Midtown (between 59th St. and 14th St.)
- Downtown (anything south of 14th St.)

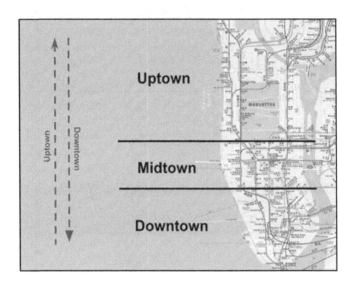

While Uptown, Midtown, and Downtown are geographic regions of Manhattan, **the words *uptown* and *downtown* can also mean your direction of travel.** If you head north or towards the Bronx or Queens, you can say you are headed "uptown"; if you head south or towards Brooklyn, you can say you are headed "downtown."

The subway map

Free subway maps are available at the ticket booths in each subway station. Many mobile applications and online maps will help you too (see the FAQ). For our purposes, let's focus on the official subway map provided by its operator, the MTA.

You can find the official map on the MTA website (http://www.mta.info/maps/submap.html). Because the map changes occasionally (e.g., due to hurricane damage, newly constructed connections, or even line extensions), be sure to get the latest map. It looks something like this:

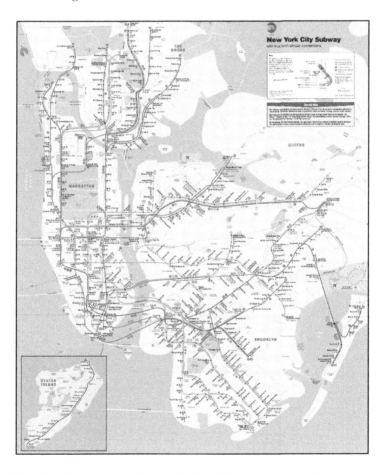

The first thing I want to point out is that **this map is not drawn to scale.** Manhattan is not that wide and Staten Island isn't really that small.

The map is intentionally distorted to highlight the subway lines, stations, and the connections between them. Stations might actually be farther apart or closer together than they appear on this map.

The thick, solid colored lines are obviously the subway lines. You can also find on this map a few of the other commuter lines that are not officially part of the subway, such as Long Island Rail Road (LIRR) tracks, buses, and AirTrains — but let's ignore those for now.

As you can see, no subway line ever leaves New York and no physical subway connection exists from Staten Island to the rest of the subway system.

Unlike many other subway systems around the world, **there are no zones** because **you pay the same fare regardless of how far or how long your trip is.** The cost of going from one station to a neighboring station (say, a one-minute ride) is the same as traveling from one end of the map to the other (which might take two hours).

The subway lines

The colored subway lines on the map indicate related trains that share a portion of common track. Here are the main lines:

Train	Line Name	Express	Local
① ② ③	Broadway - 7th Ave.	② ③	①
④ ⑤ ⑥ ⬧6	Lexington Ave. / Pelham	④ ⑤ ⬧6	⑥
⑦ ⬧7	Flushing	⬧7	⑦
Ⓐ Ⓒ Ⓔ	8th Ave.	Ⓐ	Ⓒ Ⓔ
Ⓑ Ⓓ Ⓕ Ⓜ	6th Ave.	Ⓑ Ⓓ	Ⓕ Ⓜ
Ⓝ Ⓠ Ⓡ	Broadway	Ⓠ	Ⓝ Ⓡ
Ⓙ Ⓩ	Nassau St.	Ⓩ	Ⓙ
Ⓛ	14th St. - Carnasie		Ⓛ
Ⓢ	Various shuttles		Ⓢ

Don't refer to these lines by colors. People never say, "Take the green or red line"; they say, "Take the 4, 5, and 6 or the 1, 2, and 3."

Trains of the same color share a common track at some point on their journey. However, they have different starting and/or ending stations. For instance, the 1, 2, and 3 trains all run along Broadway as well as 7th Ave. (which is why it's called the Broadway – 7th Ave. line) but the lines split at the end, creating completely different starting and ending stations (South Ferry and Van Cortland Park for the 1 train, Flatbush Ave. and Wakefield for the 2 train, and New Lots and Harlem 148th for the 3 train).

Trains are either express or local. Express trains skip certain stations for faster service, while local trains stop at every station along their path. Some trains, such as the 6 or 7, can either be express or local, which is why their icon can be either a circle (local) or a diamond (express), as shown in the previous table. Unfortunately, trains are not reliably express or local along their entire route. A single train can be an express train in Manhattan but turn local in Queens (or vice versa). For instance, the Q train is an express train in Manhattan but turns into a local train in Brooklyn.

The subway stations

Not surprisingly, subway stations appear as black and white dots on the subway lines (I explain the difference shortly). Surprisingly, however, subway station names are *not* unique. See how there are five stations named 23rd St. and four stations named 14th St. in just this area alone (you differentiate them by their subway line):

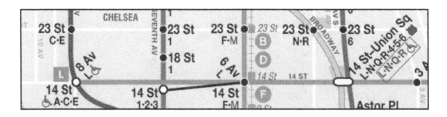

Similarly, the 86th St. station could be the one on the 4, 5, or 6 line in Manhattan or the one on the R line in Brooklyn (both stations are very far apart):

 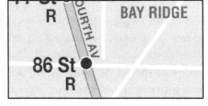

Take a look at the different meanings on the map:

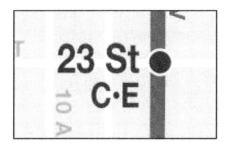

A station with a black dot means that only local trains stop here; express trains skip this station. Underneath the station name are listed the trains that stop here. In the example above, it's the C as well as E train. This makes sense because those are considered local trains.

A station with a white dot means that both the local and express trains stop at this station. In other words, *all* trains stop here *all* the time. In the example above, the express 4 and 5 trains stop here as well as the local 6 train.

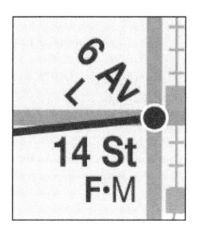

I already mentioned that station names are not unique (different stations carry the same name). Unfortunately, the reverse is true as well: the same physical station can have different names, depending on which train you are taking.

The station shown in the picture above is known as the 6th Ave. station if you are coming from the L train but it's known as the 14th St. station if you are coming from the F or M train.

You might notice that the letter *M* is not boldfaced in the picture above. Subway line names that are not boldfaced indicate stops that are not serviced around the clock. Consult the schedule online to determine when the part-time service commences or ends. For instance, the M train stops at the boldfaced stations during the weekday only (but does not stop here at night).

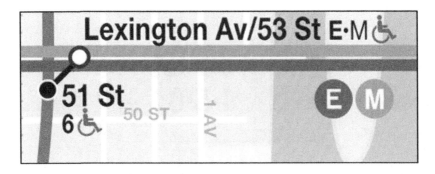

A solid black line between two stations means that there exists a physical passageway (usually a tunnel) allowing you to transfer between subway lines without leaving the subway system or requiring you to swipe your MetroCard again.

For example, three trains stop at two stations in the previous map:

- The E (from the 8th Ave. line)
- The M (from the 6th St. line)
- The 6 (from the Lexington Ave. line)

Notice how the 51st St. station is a local stop on the 6 line and how the Lexington Ave./53rd St. station is an express stop on the E and M lines.

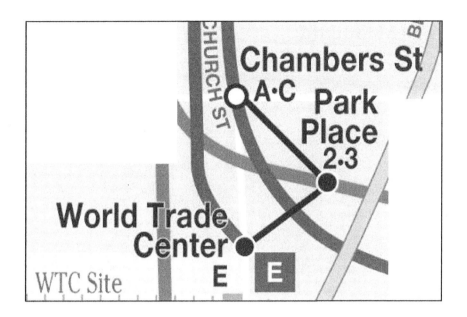

Putting this knowledge together, I hope you can deduce from this picture that the A and C trains stop at Chambers St., the 2 and 3 trains stop at Park Place, and the E train stops at the World Trade Center — and all three stations are connected to one another by free tunnels.

Don't expect to understand the New York subway map immediately, or even soon. It's a dense document conveying perhaps more information than you need to get from point A to point B. The most important things to pay attention to when looking at this map are the train numbers or letters shown below the subway station names.

The MetroCard

In order to use the subway, you need to buy a farecard, called a
MetroCard. It's the size of a credit card and made of (cheap) plastic that
looks like this (front and back):

It has a black magnetic stripe at the bottom, three rounded corners, and
one "cut off" corner.

The back of the card has a physical expiration date (usually set pretty far
in the future). This physical expiration date indicates the time when the
card becomes unusable and must be exchanged for another one at a token
booth. Don't confuse this date with the expiration of an Unlimited Ride
card. I explain that later.

There are two main types of MetroCards: Regular and Unlimited Ride.[3] They look identical, so you can't tell the difference unless you swipe them at a card reader. Regardless of the type of MetroCard, it costs $1 just to buy the card.

Children under 44 inches (112 cm.) regardless of age can ride trains for free and don't need to buy a card. (They can just walk underneath the turnstile.)

Regular MetroCard (Pay-Per-Ride)

The regular MetroCard (also known as a Pay-Per-Ride card) carries a real dollar value that decreases every time you take the subway (hence "pay per ride"). You can keep on adding value to the card whenever your balance runs low.

With this card, the cost of riding the subway is $2.50 per ride (regardless of the destination or length of the ride).

When you add more than $5 to the card, you get a 5% discount. This means that adding $5 actually adds $5.25 to your balance. In addition to the balance, the fee for the card itself is $1.

Pay-Per-Ride cards can be shared by up to four people. To share a card, swipe the card for each person individually: swipe the MetroCard, let the first person enter, swipe it again to let the next person enter, and so on.

You can combine the values of multiple Pay-Per-Ride cards by going to the information booth and asking the attendant to combine them for you. When you do so, only the current values are accumulated; the $1 fee for each card is not taken into account.

---

[3] There also exists a Single-Ride ticket for $2.75 but it is not economical to buy it.

Unlimited Ride cards

Unlimited Ride cards allow you to ride the subway as often as you want, as long as the time window that you bought for the card hasn't passed. There are only two time windows available:

- 7-Day Unlimited Ride: $30 (+ $1 fee for the card itself)
- 30-Day Unlimited Ride: $112 (+ $1 fee for the card itself)

Sorry, there aren't any weekend passes or single-day passes. If you think you are going to make more than 12 individual trips (a very likely scenario for tourists staying more than two days), buying a 7-Day Unlimited Ride card will be cheaper than paying 12 times.

The time window does not activate until you swipe the card for the very first time at a turnstile to enter the system. For instance, you can buy the card on January 17, activate it on April 1, and it will expire at midnight between April 7 and April 8.

Unlimited cards always expire exactly at midnight on the 7th or 30th day, regardless of the time you activated the card on the first day. For instance, if you activate a 7-Day Unlimited Ride card on Monday morning, it will expire Sunday night at midnight. If you activate the card Monday evening at 11:30pm, it *still* expires Sunday night at midnight. As a result, you effectively get to use it only for 6 days and 30 minutes. In that case, you are better off paying for a single ride using the Pay-Per-Ride card and then activating the Unlimited Ride card the next morning.

Unlimited Ride cards cannot be shared by two people. In fact, there is an 18-minute delay between each swipe to prevent the card from being used by more than one person.

As I noted before, on the back of every MetroCard is printed a physical expiration date. Do not confuse the printed physical card expiration date with the paid expiration of the Unlimited Ride time window.

A card can carry both time and value

A card can carry "time," "value," **or both.** In other words, you can add a dollar value to an Unlimited Ride card or buy time to an existing Pay-Per-Ride card. When this happens, the **time card always takes precedence** when you swipe it at a turnstile (it will activate the time window as necessary). After the time portion of the card has expired, it will then (and *only* then) start draining the value of your card.

Buying a MetroCard

You can buy a MetroCard at any subway station, either at a ticket booth or MetroCard vending machine located inside the subway station. They look like this:

The screen on the machine does not have the most intuitive layout. I've devised the following **simplified** flowchart to navigate this machine:

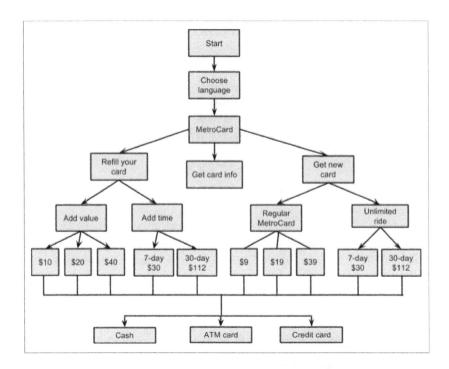

Remember that in addition to the price listed above, you must add $1 for the card itself.

When you pay with cash, note that change is always provided in $1 coins.

When you pay by credit card, the machine will ask you for the ZIP code associated with your account. If you come from outside the United States, leave the field blank and press OK.

A step-by-step guide to using the subway system

Now that you have a basic understanding of the subway lines, stations, and map, let's move on to the fun part: taking an actual trip! I assume that you can plot out a general plan of how to get to your destination. This might involve deciding the following:

- Which station am I entering?
- Which station am I exiting?
- Which combination of trains should I take?
- In which direction should I take each train?

There are many ways to get from point A to point B. Your trip will likely involve taking a few trains and making one or two transfers. Make sure that the stations you are eyeing are served by the trains you intend to take.

Step 1: Finding and entering the subway station

Most of the time, you can recognize subway stations by the green or green-white "globe lamps" that surround the subway entrances:

Subway entrances can be hidden inside large buildings and shopping entrances, so look carefully:

Use your physical map or the map on your mobile phone (or ask a local) to find the closest subway station.

Sometimes it's beneficial to walk to a station that is farther away to catch a more convenient line depending on where your final destination is.

Because subway trains are really long, subway stations may have many entrances and exits. **Not all entrances are created equal.** Exit-only staircases are marked with a solid red globe.

You can't enter this station through these stairs; you have to find the other entrances instead.[4]

More importantly, some entrances can only be used to access trains in certain directions. This is clearly stated on the sign above the entrance.

---

[4] Sometimes there are red globes around an exit that you *can* enter as long as you already carry a MetroCard. It is not possible to tell this from street level, though; you just learn this from experience.

This is an entrance to the 28th St. station on the N and R line. However, you can catch the N and R trains only in the **downtown direction** from this entrance. For uptown service, you have to find the corresponding uptown entrance. Because subway lines generally run underneath the streets in Manhattan, you can often find uptown train entrances on the east side of the street and downtown train entrances on the west side. (Imagine the trains running on the same side of the street as the cars above them.)

You can catch the Downtown 6 train from this entrance to the Canal St. station. You can also catch the J, Z, N, Q, and R trains (in all directions) from this entrance via a free passageway (tunnels).

In case you didn't notice the red globe I mentioned earlier, this staircase is an exit only. You cannot enter the subway from here; you have to find another entrance to this station nearby.

Step 2: Going through the turnstile

Before entering the subway system, you have to swipe your MetroCard at the turnstile:

Before entering the turnstile, be sure that this is the right place to enter. Notice in the picture above that this is the entry only for the downtown and Brooklyn-bound train. For uptown service, you have to find another entrance. In some stations, once you are in, it's impossible to get to the other side of the platform without leaving the subway again. This means you might have to wait 18 minutes before your Unlimited Ride MetroCard becomes usable again or pay again with the Pay-Per-Ride card!

Besides the turnstile, you can enter a station through the revolving doors:

In both cases, you will find a card reader on your right side. Have your MetroCard ready as you approach the card reader. (New Yorkers hate it when people fumble for their card.) Here is how to swipe your card against the card reader:

Make sure the magnetic stripe faces down and toward you. Once you swipe the card, the display tells you that you can go and will also display the Unlimited Ride card's expiration date[5] or the remaining value balance.

---

[5] To be exact, the Unlimited Ride time window will expire at 11:59 p.m. on the displayed date.

If the machine can't read the card, it will ask you to swipe the card again. Most tourists fail because they swipe too slowly. Don't swipe the card too quickly either. Watch how the locals do it. If you fail to swipe properly, don't try your luck at another turnstile. Keep trying to swipe at the same turnstile. Trying at another turnstile might render your card useless for 18 minutes because it thinks you have already used it.

Once you enter the system, you can put your MetroCard away. You won't need it to exit.

Step 3: Finding the right platform

I assume you already know which train you want to take. You should also know by now the direction of the train you want (uptown, downtown, Manhattan-bound, Brooklyn-bound, etc.). Knowing this allows you to follow the simple signs with the arrows to guide you to your platform:

All directional signs have arrows. These signs tell you in which direction to walk to get *where* you want to go. The arrow applies to the entire sign — so in the picture immediately above, the sign tells you to go downstairs to catch the Uptown B, D, F, and M trains as well as the Uptown 6 train.

Now that you've reached the platform, there are signs that tell you on which side of the platform to stand:

Finally, confirm that you are standing on the correct side of the platform. Look at the signs that are parallel to the train's track and **do not have any arrows.** They look like this:

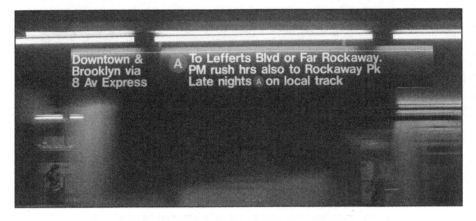

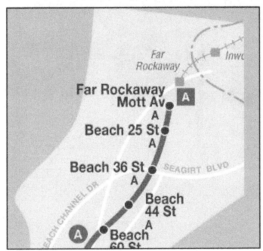

As you can see, these signs tell you the train designation (A), the train's direction (downtown), but more importantly **the name of the very last station of the train.** By looking at the very last station of a particular train on the map, you can determine whether that train is going in the right direction for you.

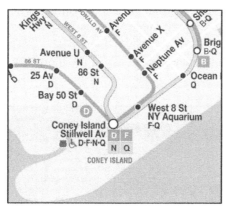

Remember that signs with arrows do *not* indicate the platform you are standing on. This confuses tourists all the time. They see the following sign and think that the A, C, E, and 7 trains (or 1, 2, 3, 4, and S trains) stop here:

Instead, these signs are telling them to keep walking to the left or right to reach those trains.

Step 4: Waiting for the train

With the exception of the C and G trains, most trains are long enough to cover an entire platform. It therefore doesn't matter where you stand on the platform.

Although trains *do* run on set schedules (http://www.mta.info/schedules/), it probably suffices to just go down into the station and wait for the next train, which should arrive anywhere between 2–5 minutes during rush hour and 10–15 minutes at night. The subway runs 24 hours per day and never closes. (You've heard that New York never sleeps, haven't you?) You could catch a train at 4 a.m. if you wanted to, although the wait might be long.

Some train lines (unfortunately too few at the moment) are equipped to indicate how long you have to wait for the next train(s):

These displays tell you the order of trains (1st, 2nd, 3rd, 4th, etc.); the train line (5, 1, and 2); the last station and, hence, direction of the train (Bowling Green, 14th St., Flatbush Ave.); and the estimated arrival time. Some displays also tell you the side of the platform you should expect the train to arrive on (the 14th St.-bound train on the left, the Flatbush-bound train on the right).

The first line always displays the next approaching train (1.), whereas the second line will alternate between all subsequent trains (2., 3., 4., etc.). If the first line turns yellow and is blinking, it means that the train just entered the station.

Step 5: Entering the train car

Because a single platform can service different trains, you want to confirm that an approaching train is indeed the train you are waiting for.

Trains carry the train line designation at the front of the train:

On the side of the train, you will likely see both the name of the line and the name of the last station:

Once the train car's doors open, **let passengers exit first before you enter**. Once you enter the car, **be sure to walk all the way in to let others behind you come in as well**. Trains can be very crowded during rush hour. It's normal to find yourself sandwiched between people.

The first thing to do after entering a car is to look for the route map that indicates the stations you will encounter on the line. Sometimes, the route maps are just simple printed signs:

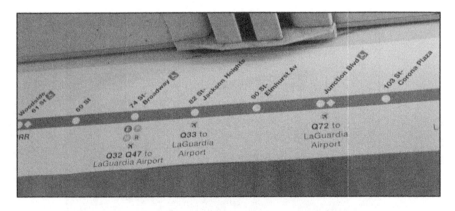

Below some station names on this map are other connections that you can take. For example, at 74th St.–Broadway, you can connect to the E, F, M and R trains as well as take the Q32 or Q47 bus to the airport.

Some route maps are fancier displays:

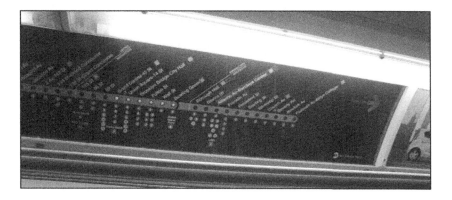

The large lighted arrow on the end indicates the direction of travel. Yellow lights indicate subway stations that are coming up. I took this picture on a train from the 59th St. station to Grand Central–42nd St. The last stop of this train is Bowling Green. When the train enters Grand Central station, that first yellow light will also blink.

On fancier trains, you might even see an LED display indicating the upcoming stations:

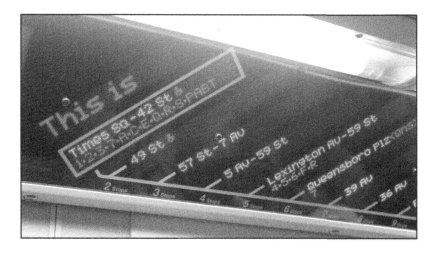

Here we are at Times Square, where you can transfer for free to the 1, 2, 3, 7, A, C, E, Q, R, and S trains, and also walk to the Port Authority Bus Terminal (PABT). The next station is 49th St. The display keeps on updating (shifting left) as you travel.

At last, overhead displays also tell you the next station:

These displays will alternate between the following information:

1. <Time> ("10:18am")
2. To <last station> ("To Coney Island")
3. "The next stop is"
4. <next stop> ("28 St")

Step 6: Exiting the train

Besides the station displays I previously mentioned, the driver will also announce the upcoming station name, although hearing (and understanding) the announcement is another matter. Look out the window to determine the station as well:

After you leave the subway car, follow the signs with the arrows to transfer to another line or follow the red exit signs to leave the subway system altogether. As you go through the turnstiles or revolving doors again to exit the system, you won't have to swipe your MetroCard.

When you finally exit the subway station, you might not immediately know your bearings. Here are two recommendations to help you out:

- Right before you exit the subway station, look at all the exits available. Usually those exits are marked as NW exit, SW exit, NE exit, SE exit. If you know where you want to go on the map, these clues can help you leave at the most convenient exit.
- Look for landmarks. By remembering that the Chrysler building and Empire State building is in Midtown and that the new One World Trade Center is downtown, you can deduce your relative location based on where you spot these landmarks.

When the system doesn't work as expected

So far, so good. Confusing as the system already is, it's going to get even more confusing as you watch out for some caveats.

A train temporarily replaces another line

Occasionally an express train is rerouted to a local track (or vice versa) — or even rerouted to a completely other subway line altogether. For instance, the 4 or 5 trains, which typically run on the Lexington Line on the east side of Manhattan, sometimes run on the 7th Ave. line on the west side of Manhattan. Somewhere downtown it forks from the usual 4/5 line and merges back eventually to the 4/5 line somewhere uptown.

For instance, you find yourself standing at Times Square and suddenly see the 4 or 5 train approaching on the side of the platform where you otherwise would expect the 2 or 3 train. The conductor's announcement should be something like, "This is a 4/5 train running on the 2/3 line." In those cases, just think of that train as a 2 or 3 train. However, eventually the train will merge back to its original track and you might find some temporary sign posted in the station indicating when this will happen. Pay close attention to the conductor's announcement; it'll let you know when the train goes back to its original line.

On older trains, the route map shows a warning light, indicating that it's incorrect:

Evening service

In the evening — usually after 10, 11, or midnight — you'll see some subtle changes to the trains. They arrive less frequently and run more slowly than usual. Express trains tend to become local, meaning that they stop at every station. You can find exactly what happens to your line by looking at the MTA website (http://www.mta.info/nyct/service/). Consult the late-night subway map (http://www.mta.info/maps/) too.

Weekend service

Because the subway system operates 24/7 for all 365 days of the year, maintenance of the tracks or construction has to be done while the system is in operation. New lines are currently being added, while existing tracks and stations require constant maintenance. To avoid disrupting rush-hour traffic, maintenance happens on weekends — and they happen *every* weekend. In fact, it's such a common occurrence that the MTA website changes its home page every weekend to "The Weekender" edition that indicates what kinds of changes you can expect.

As you enter stations, you will find "Planned Service Changes" indicating the type of change:

The type of change is very specific. Read those leaflets carefully to determine what your next options are. The most common type of changes are as follows:

Express turns local

Express trains turn local for a certain section. This isn't too bad because you can still use the same train to get to the same destination. You just have to endure stopping at every station that usually would be skipped.

Local turns express

A local train that usually stops at every station is now an express train for a certain section. This usually means that in order to exit at your desired local station, you have to take this express train to the next express stop and then catch a local train in the opposite direction to end up at your desired destination.

Train is complemented with a bus

The train is no longer running. You have to exit the subway station and take a free shuttle bus that drives along the same route to each subway station. This takes longer since above-ground traffic tends be slower.

Train doesn't run altogether

This train is out of service. Find some other route using a combination of other trains to get to your final destination.

Miscellaneous information

Stay in the know:

- A few stations — not many, but they are increasing — have cell phone service and free Wi-Fi.
- If a particular car on a train is unusually empty, compared to others, there's probably a very good reason for this. Don't board that car unless you are prepared to see something really disgusting.
- The subway is more than 100 years old. It can be dirty and smelly down there. Don't be surprised to see rats crawling around the tracks and occasionally even at the ends of platforms.
- Platforms and tunnels are not air-conditioned.[6] The heat becomes unbearable in summer.
- When you travel in a group, make sure everyone hops onto the train at the same time. Don't run ahead and catch a connecting train or you might leave some members of your party behind.
- Don't walk between the cars of a train. It is illegal and dangerous.
- If you find yourself accidentally dropping something valuable onto the tracks while waiting for the train, never retrieve the item yourself. The third rail on the track is electrified. It's not unheard of for people to be killed by an oncoming train. Notify a station agent in the station booths; he or she can notify someone else to retrieve the item for you properly.
- Don't be afraid to ask a New Yorker for help. Contrary to popular belief, we are actually pretty nice and helpful. We just won't offer any help unless we're asked.

---

[6] The new stations being built for the 2nd Ave. and 7 line extensions will be air-conditioned.

Subway etiquette

There are some unspoken rules of etiquette to follow when you ride the subway. They may not be all that different from other transportation systems' ridership rules, but allow me to state them here:

- Don't stop suddenly in the middle of a stairway or hallway to talk or text on your mobile phone. You'll annoy those behind you.
- When you ride an escalator, stand to the right so others can walk past you on the left.
- When you approach a turnstile, have your MetroCard ready to swipe.
- If you can't successfully swipe your MetroCard three times, be courteous and let some people behind you enter first before you try again.
- Let passengers exit the train first by standing to the left or right of the opening door.
- When you enter a train, be sure to walk all the way into the train. Do not stop at the entrance and block other people behind you from entering the car.
- Do not hold the doors open for others. You will delay the train (and the trains behind you) and annoy your fellow riders.
- Do not lean on the poles inside the train. People will want to hold on to them.
- Don't eat food that others can smell on the train (no matter how good it smells).
- Don't stare at people. It makes us New Yorkers uncomfortable.
- Give up your seat for an elderly or pregnant women.
- On crowded trains, don't put your backpack or handbag on a seat that otherwise could be used by someone else.
- On crowded trains, don't wear backpacks on the back. Wear them in front or take them off altogether.
- As you exit the subway, don't stop at the top of the stairway and admire the scenery. There are people behind you who need to exit as well.

Frequently asked questions

- **Is it safe to ride the subway?**
  Generally, yes. Violence and crime on the subway peaked in the 1980s. Today New York City continues to be one of the largest safe cities in the world. This isn't Paris; there generally *aren't* any pickpockets to worry about.

- **What mobile apps do you recommend?**
  There are tons of them. Popular ones include HopStop (http://www.hopstop.com/), Embark (http://letsembark.com/), NYCMate (http://matemate.com/citymates/nycmate), and Episode6's NYC Bus & Subway map (http://www.episode6.com). You can also go on Google Maps (which displays the expected time of arrival of trains when you click or tap on station names), transitme.com, or use MTA's official Trip Planner (http://tripplanner.mta.info).

- **What else can I use the MetroCard for?**
  You can use your MetroCard to pay for local bus rides. It's the same fare as the subway, so if you have an Unlimited Ride card, it's essentially free. If you have a Pay-Per-Ride card, it will cost you $2.50 per ride. However, there is a free transfer from the subway (and vice versa), so if you just used your Pay-Per-Ride card for a subway ride, you can transfer to a bus for free within two hours. If you have used the Pay-Per-Ride card for multiple people on the subway, you have to swipe the card only once on a bus. The display will tell you that there are multiple free transfers and the bus driver will let multiple people go through.

  You can also use your MetroCard to take the short (three-minute) tramway from Manhattan to Roosevelt Island, which gives you some nice views over Manhattan. Because it participates in the one-fare system, it's essentially free if you have an Unlimited Ride card. The same concept about transfers, described above, applies here as well if you use a Per-Per-Ride card.

- **Is it OK to take a bike onto a subway car?**

  Yes, although on crowded trains you might get some stares.

- **Can I take luggage onto trains?**

  Many tourists do that, but you should consider several things. First, it might be strenuous to carry large pieces of luggage up and down the stairs. Some escalators are very narrow and some elevators have an unwelcome smell. Second, avoid bringing large pieces of luggage with you during rush hour. You might get some stares by commuters on crowded trains.

  Carry-on luggage fits neatly underneath a turnstile, so you can just walk through the turnstile with it. For larger pieces of luggage, however, you'll need the help of an attendant in a ticket booth to enter. First swipe your MetroCard at a turnstile, then manually rotate the turnstile with your hand **without going through it**. After the attendant has seen you do that, he or she will then remotely release the Emergency Exit door that is usually located next to the turnstile.

  Following this procedure, you can easily go through the door while properly paying for your trip. To exit the subway, simply push against the metal bar of the Emergency Exit door to open it. Don't worry about activating the emergency siren; simply walk through the door with your luggage and the sound will eventually stop.

- **Are the subway stations handicap-accessible?**

  Because the subway was built long before the passage of the Americans with Disabilities Act (ADA), a large majority of subway stations are not easily accessible for people with disabilities. Not all stations have elevators, and the majority of them don't even have escalators. Although the MTA is trying to improve the situation, it will take a long time. See the accessibility page of the MTA website (http://web.mta.info/accessibility/stations.htm) for information about which stations are ADA-accessible (97 out of 468, as of 2013). On the subway map, ADA-accessible stations are identified with a wheelchair icon. You can also see those icons on the route maps inside the trains.

- **Is there really a hidden subway station?**

  The City Hall subway station is an abandoned station below City Hall in downtown Manhattan that features very beautiful architecture. Due to the station's tight curvature, however, it can no longer service today's long trains. It was closed in 1945 and is generally inaccessible to tourists. However, there is a way to see some parts of this hidden subway station. Simply take the 6 local train heading downtown into the Brooklyn Bridge/City Hall station. The automated announcement will inform you that this is the last station and that you must exit the train. If you remain on the train regardless, it will continue to pass through a closed-off, original section of the City Hall subway station to make a U-turn back to the same Brooklyn Bridge/City Hall station, where it's now the uptown 6 train. As the train passes through the closed station, you will see the (often well-lit) remnants of the original City Hall station on the right-hand side. You'll get only a brief glimpse of this station's platform. To admire the real beauty of this station, you have to become a member of the New York Transit Museum and go on one of their occasional tours of the station.

Getting into Manhattan from the airports

Three major airports cover the greater New York metropolitan area:

- **John F. Kennedy International Airport** (JFK) located in Brooklyn
- **LaGuardia Airport** (LGA) located in Queens
- **Newark Liberty International Airport** (EWR) located in Newark, New Jersey

Unfortunately, none of these three airports is conveniently located. It's always somewhat painful to get into Manhattan from these airports. The following sections outline the most popular ways of reaching Manhattan. All modes of transportation take at least 30 minutes.

If you have a lot of luggage, taking a cab is generally the most convenient way to get to Manhattan. You won't have to take multiple trains, ride elevators, or climb stairs. However, cabs can be very expensive and oftentimes take much longer than public transportation, especially during rush hour.

If you decide to take a cab, be wary of people standing inside the baggage claim area who offer you transportation to the city. It's illegal and somewhat of a scam. Always go to the official taxi stands outside the baggage claim area. The yellow cabs there aren't just famous, they're the real deal. As for tipping your cabbie, please note that the credit card machines in taxi cabs usually provide you with a default choice of a 20% tip. You can change this manually to a more standard tip of 10–15%.

John F. Kennedy International Airport (JFK)

JFK has one of the best train and railroad connections into the city. You have many options and the prices and total travel times are fairly predictable and consistent.

Option 1: Taxi cab
Price: $52 + tip; duration: 50 minutes

Taking a cab from JFK into Manhattan incurs a flat fee of $52 plus toll and tip. Because of the flat fee, you do not have to negotiate with the cab driver (and the driver does not even start the meter). However, to avoid being ripped off, you should reconfirm this flat fee policy before your ride. The ride might take you about 50 minutes (depending on traffic and destination).

Option 2: Airport express shuttle
Price: $16; duration: 1 hour

As you exit the terminal, look for white buses that say "NYCAirporter.com". They drop you off either at Grand Central station or the Port Authority Bus Terminal in Manhattan.

Option 3: AirTrain and Long Island Rail Road
Price: $5 AirTrain + $7/$9.50 for LIRR; duration: 1 hour

The Long Island Rail Road (LIRR) consists of commuter trains that bring workers from outside the city into Manhattan. Because they are for commuters, you will find that they run frequently and can be very convenient. During rush hour on weekdays, there are trains going to New York's Pennsylvania ("Penn") Station almost every 5–10 minutes.

The LIRR station near the JFK airport is called the Jamaica Station, but it takes 15–20 minutes just to get to that station. From the terminal, follow the signs to the AirTrain shuttle:

The AirTrain is an elevated, fully automated train that connects the different terminals and parking garages. It looks like this:

The AirTrain has two final destinations (Howard Beach & Jamaica Station). Even though it's technically possible to get into Manhattan from either station, it's generally faster to take the route that goes through Jamaica Station. Look for the overhead monitors to wait for a train that is labeled "Jamaica Train":

You don't pay to enter the AirTrain; you pay when you exit. Take the AirTrain to its very last stop at Jamaica Station (this ride alone might take up to 20 minutes).

As you exit the AirTrain at Jamaica Station, you will find turnstiles as well as MetroCard vending machines:

This is where you need to buy an AirTrain MetroCard in the amount of $5. Please note that **you cannot buy Unlimited Ride MetroCards for the NYC subway system here.** The MetroCards you buy here are strictly for the AirTrain. (Although the machines offer and advertise a combined ticket for $7.25 that includes a single-use ticket for the subway, it's not worth it.)

After you swipe the AirTrain MetroCard to exit the AirTrain system through the automated turnstiles, follow the crowds to turn left onto the bridge over to the Long Island Railroad (LIRR) trains:

Taking the Long Island Rail Road (LIRR) train from here is very convenient, especially during rush hour (trains go to New York's Pennsylvania Station almost every 5–10 minutes). From the displays, you can determine the next train to Penn Station, the track where you can board, and whether the trip would be considered peak or off-peak.

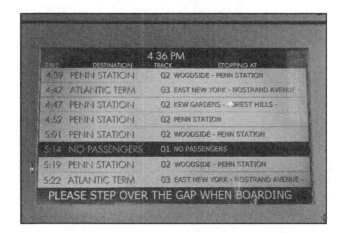

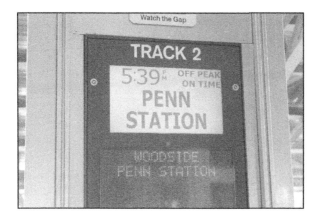

With that information in mind, you can then buy the appropriate one-way ticket from one of these machines ($7 for off-peak, $9.50 for peak time).

The LIRR train ride from here into Penn Station lasts about 25 minutes and might make a few stops before it arrives there. Once at Penn Station, try to remember the area where the LIRR trains arrive. Penn Station is an immensely dense and highly confusing rail station that serves a multitude of trains. You'll want to remember the LIRR train area in case you want to take the LIRR back to the airport.

Option 4: AirTrain and subway

Price: $5 AirTrain + price of subway MetroCard; duration: 1½ hour

Since it's likely that you'll buy an Unlimited Ride MetroCard for the New York subway trains anyway, you might as well take this travel package and use the subway trains to get into Manhattan from here.

Unfortunately the subway system does not go directly to the airport. You have to take the AirTrain from the terminal to the LIRR's Jamaica Station first, so follow the steps described previously in Option 3 to get to Jamaica Station. Instead of taking the LIRR trains, however, simply walk past all the LIRR trains towards the end of the bridge until you see the elevators:

Take an elevator to the bottom floor (Level A), where you will enter the **Sutphin Blvd./Archer Ave./JFK Airport** subway station, which is served by the E, J, and Z trains.

Here you can buy your Unlimited Ride MetroCards for the subway. At this point, you are often approached by strangers trying to sell you used MetroCards. Don't buy their cards; buy them from the official machines.

From this station, take the next Manhattan-bound E Train (final destination World Trade Center). The trip from here into Manhattan can take up to 45 minutes.

LaGuardia Airport (LGA)

Even though LaGuardia Airport is the closest airport to Manhattan, it does not offer any train or railroad connection to Manhattan.

Option 1: Taxi cab
Price: $35–$50; duration: 30 minutes

Unlike the JFK airport, there is no flat fee to take a cab from LaGuardia. You are going to have to pay the metered fare, which can fluctuate a lot depending on the exact location of your destination and how bad traffic is.

Option 2: Airport Express shuttle
Price: $13; duration: 40 minutes

Follow the "Express Bus to Manhattan" signs and look for the white "NYCAirporter.com" buses. Those buses cost $13 from the airport and drop you off either at Grand Central station, Port Authority Bus Station, or Penn Station in Manhattan. They look like this:

Option 3: Q70 Bus
Price: Price of subway fare; duration: 40 minutes

Since it's likely that you'll buy an Unlimited Ride MetroCard for the New York subway trains anyway, which provides you with free access to the public bus system, you can take the Q70 bus to get to the nearest subway station.

First, follow the signs to the "Public Bus to Manhattan":

Right before you exit the terminal, you will also find a New York subway vending machine:

Here you can, and should, buy your Unlimited MetroCard. This is the same card that you will be using for both the bus and all subway trains in New York.

There are multiple public buses that serve LaGuardia, so be sure to look for the one labeled "Q70":

The bus takes about 20 minutes and arrives at the **74th St./Broadway/Jackson Hts./Roosevelt Ave.** subway station in Queens, served by the E and 7 trains. From here, take the next Manhattan-bound E train (about another 20 minutes to Midtown).

Newark Liberty International Airport (EWR)

The Newark airport is the farthest airport from New York City. In fact, it's located in the neighboring state of New Jersey. However, it's close enough that many New York City–bound flights land here as well.

Option 1: Taxi cab
Price: $70–90; duration: 50–70 minutes

Naturally, the cost of taking a cab from the Newark airport is very expensive. Because the cab has to pass through a few tollbooths, you'll end up spending about $90, including tip. Traffic into New York through the tunnels can take some time, too, so it's not always the most convenient way.

Option 2: Newark Airport Express shuttle
Price: $16; duration: 50–70 minutes

The Newark Airport Express shuttle runs every 15–30 minutes. There can be a bit of a wait for all passengers to board the bus and pay their fare, so the wait alone can add some time to your trip.

Follow the signs to the buses to New York City:

The bus itself looks like this:

You can pay with cash or credit card on the bus. The bus trip itself takes about 30–40 minutes to reach Manhattan. It drops you off at the Port Authority Bus Terminal, Bryant Park, or Grand Central station.

Option 3: AirTrain and New Jersey Transit
Price: $12.75; duration: 30–50 minutes

The New Jersey Transit (often abbreviated "NJ Transit") is a commuter train serving the Newark airport. Because this train comes at set times and is not subject to traffic, it is often the fastest way to get into New York City during the weekday. However, it runs infrequently at night or on weekends. I usually take the NJ Transit when I arrive during the weekday and the Newark Airport Express bus at night or on weekends.

In order to get to the NJ Transit stop, you first have to take the AirTrain (an elevated, fully automated train system that connects the different terminals). Follow the signs to the AirTrain:

The AirTrain entrances are easily recognizable inside the terminals:

You don't pay to enter the AirTrain; you pay when you exit. There are two directions for the AirTrain. Take the one labeled "RAILink":

Take the AirTrain to its last stop (Rail Link Terminal). There you can buy tickets for the NJ Transit at these machines:

The ticket into New York City costs $12.50. Use the ticket to go through the turnstiles, but hold on to the ticket; you'll need it later.

Follow the signs to Track 1, A (New York and Newark). You can then wait at the platform for the next train into New York ("New York-SEC"):

Once you are on the NJ Transit, a conductor will ask to see your NJ Transit ticket again (he or she will also probably keep the ticket). You won't need the ticket to exit.

The NJ Transit makes a few stops before it reaches New York. One of the stops might be Newark Penn Station. Do not confuse Newark Penn Station with the final destination, New York Penn Station (they sound similar).

As you exit Penn Station in New York, try to remember where the NJ Transit area is. As I mentioned before, Penn Station is a highly confusing and chaotic station serving multiple trains. You'll want to remember where the NJ Transit area is in case you want to take it back to the airport. If you do use the NJ Transit to get back to the airport, you will need to use your NJ Transit ticket twice: first to show it to the conductor on the train, and second to enter the Newark AirTrain system to get to the airport terminals.

Afterword

I hope you enjoyed reading this guide as much as I enjoyed writing it. I really hope this guide is useful for tourists and first-time visitors, and I ask that you share this guide with others. I've spent many weeks running around in the subway system taking pictures and writing this guide, and I would love to see this guide reach its intended audience. I encourage you to ask questions or provide feedback via e-mail so that I can improve this guide over time.

Despite some of my gripes about the New York subway, I do think it's one of the best subway systems in the world. It certainly provides the most bang for your buck. It's impossible to think of New York City without picturing the subway. The subway system brings a lot of jobs to the city, and is the one place where you encounter people of all races, ethnicities, genders, types, and income brackets. New York wouldn't be this great of a city were it not for its subway system.

Happy traveling!

Minh T. Nguyen
minh@minh.org

PS: I want to thank Stefan Gruenwedel for the thorough copy-editing.